T0012348

The Great Salt Lake Food Chains

The Great Salt Lake Food Chains

Fragility and Resiliency

Bonnie K. Baxter

The University of Utah Press
Salt Lake City

Publication of this edition is made possible in part by The Wallace Stegner Center for Land, Resources and the Environment, S. J. Quinney College of Law and by The Tanner Trust Fund, Special Collections Department, J. Willard Marriott Library

Copyright © 2024 by The University of Utah Press. All rights reserved.

This lecture was originally delivered on March 16, 2023, at the 28th annual symposium of the Wallace Stegner Center for Land, Resources and the Environment. The symposium is supported by the R. Harold Burton Foundation, the founding and lead donor since 1996, and by the Cultural Vision Fund and The Nature Conservancy.

The Defiance House Man colophon is a registered trademark of the University of Utah Press. It is based on a four-foot-tall Ancient Puebloan pictograph (late PIII) near Glen Canyon, Utah.

LIBRARY OF CONGRESS CATALOGING-IN-PUBLICATION DATA
Names: Baxter, Bonnie K., author. | University of Utah. Wallace Stegner
    Center for Land, Resources and the Environment. Annual Symposium (28th
    : 2023 : Salt Lake City, Utah)
Title: The Great Salt Lake food chains : fragility and resiliency / Bonnie
    K. Baxter.
Other titles: Fragility and resiliency
Identifiers: LCCN 2023049646 | ISBN 9781647691820 (paperback) | ISBN
    9781647691837 (ebook)
Subjects: LCSH: Food chains (Ecology)—Utah—Great Salt Lake. | Salt lake
    ecology—Utah—Great Salt Lake. | Resilience (Ecology)—Utah—Great Salt
    Lake. | Great Salt Lake (Utah)—Environmental conditions.
Classification: LCC F832.G7 B39 2023 | DDC
    577/.160979242—dc23/eng/20231122
LC record available at https://lccn.loc.gov/2023049646

Cover photo by Scott Baxter.
Errata and further information on this and other titles available at UofUpress.com
Printed and bound in the United States of America.

FOREWORD

The Wallace Stegner Lecture serves as a public forum for addressing the critical environmental issues that confront society. Conceived in 2009 on the centennial of Wallace Stegner's birth, the lecture honors the Pulitzer Prize–winning author, educator, and conservationist by bringing a prominent scholar, public official, advocate, or spokesperson to the University of Utah with the aim of informing and promoting public dialogue over the relationship between humankind and the natural world. The lecture is delivered in connection with the Wallace Stegner Center's annual symposium and published by the University of Utah Press to ensure broad distribution. Just as Wallace Stegner envisioned a more just and sustainable world, the lecture acknowledges Stegner's enduring conservation legacy by giving voice to "the geography of hope" that he evoked so eloquently throughout his distinguished career.

The 2023 Wallace Stegner Lecture delivered by Bonnie K. Baxter is titled "The Great Salt Lake Food Chains: Fragility and Resiliency."

Robert B. Keiter, Director
WALLACE STEGNER CENTER FOR LAND,
RESOURCES AND THE ENVIRONMENT

G reat Salt Lake persists as one of the most significant bodies of water in the western United States for migratory birds, an enormous inland sea that provides food and haven for avian travelers. A site of hemispheric importance, this saline lake is one of the largest in the world, with a salinity gradient that spans from brackish wetlands to salt-saturated brine.[1] Great Salt Lake is alluring in its simplicity and arresting in its significance, featuring simple food chains that support ten million birds annually.[2]

The organisms that live in the lake are inexorably linked to its water chemistry and salinity levels. Since Great Salt Lake has a similar salt composition to the ocean, dominated by sodium chloride, it is referred to as a thalassohaline lake.[3] As a terminal lake, it accepts water inflows but has no outflow, thus evaporation and precipitation cycles are substantial players in the lake elevation. Vacillating lake levels cause the salinity to fluctuate when elevated precipitation dilutes the brine or drought concentrates it. Typically, salinity at Great Salt Lake varies inversely with lake elevation.[4]

It is the nature of this terminal lake and its relationship to humans that has led to a frightening scenario. Overuse of upstream water and changes in the climate have combined to accelerate the shrinking of Great Salt Lake, impacting the ecology in dramatic ways. As the concentration of salt rises with the loss of water, the biology struggles to survive. This text explores the fragile food chains of the lake and examines the baked-in flexibility of life adapted to an extreme ecosystem. The situation is dire, but the lake's biology is resilient and can recover if we can bring more water to the basin in a timely manner.

THE NATURAL GREAT SALT LAKE SYSTEM

Great Salt Lake occupies the bottom of the Bonneville Basin in the Great Basin watershed in North America.[5] For the last 800,000 years, the water level has fluctuated in this terminal system but has mostly remained at an elevation similar to this modern lake.[6] The water level rose to fill the lake basin four times,[7] most recently during the last ice age, 30 to 15,000 years ago, when Lake Bonneville expanded into northwestern Utah, with its freshwater extending into eastern Nevada and southern Idaho[8] (fig. 1). As the planet entered the Holocene epoch, warming temperatures evaporated water, lowered the shoreline, and concentrated the salts. Over a few thousand years, this process produced the much-smaller Great Salt Lake, which arrived at its current level about 13,000 years ago.[9]

As modern Great Salt Lake was forming, water was abundant in nearby aquifers and springs, and the first people of Utah roamed the shorelines.[10] Early human interactions with the lake are evident in the ancient caves, artifacts, and burials in the surrounding cliffs and wetlands. Salt collected from the brine was likely a trade commodity.[11] For the last millennium, until the Euro-American ideology of manifest destiny impacted the Indigenous communities of the West, several groups of people occupied the region surrounding Great Salt Lake. To the north the Shoshone hunted and relied upon the marsh and springs near the edges of the lake. The southern shoreline was the aboriginal territory of Ute, Goshute, and Paiute.[12] Their oral histories suggest a strong relationship to the desert-like landscape.

The first written documentation of the natural history of the lake was completed by Frémont and Stansbury, working for the U.S. government. In 1843, explorer John C. Frémont mapped the topography of the lake and investigated the mineral content and biology of its waters, including brine shrimp and flies.[13] In 1849 and 1850, Captain Howard Stansbury circumnavigated Great Salt Lake to map its margins and islands. He described the lake's biology in more detail.[14] These early researchers noted a distinctive feature of

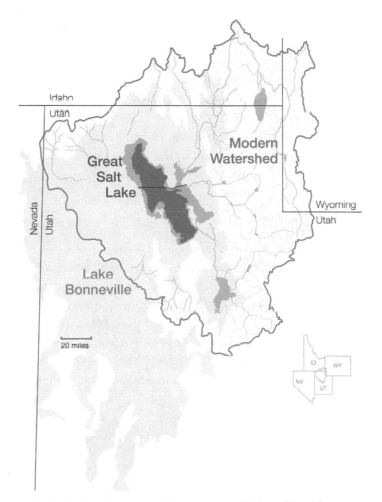

Figure 1. Great Salt Lake in the context of the current watershed in yellow and ancient Lake Bonneville in pale blue. The dark color is the 2022 historic low elevation, compared to the lighter lake average elevation. Illustration by Sheila A. Homburger.

a terminal basin: the lake level fluctuates naturally due to differences between inflows and evaporation.

Scientists in the late 1800s and early 1900s applied their modern tools to the lake water to better understand salinity, microbiology, and the life cycles in the brine.[15] For example, Josephine Tilden performed the first systematic study of algae as part of a team exploring the science of western landscapes like Yellowstone and Great Salt Lake. The mapping and the science of the water did not change the lake, but the influx of people into Utah did. The twentieth century brought enormous changes and interventions to Great Salt Lake. The natural watershed would cease to exist, but the lake ecosystem would persist, even in the face of immense disruption.

An Altered Lake System

As westward expansion continued, the human population increased along the Wasatch Front and so did their impacts to Great Salt Lake. The actions that have had the greatest consequence were upstream water diversions for human use (e.g., industry, housing, agriculture), which prevented water from reaching the lake.[16] An estimated 45 percent of the inflow from the lake's three major rivers is restricted in this way, exposing about half of the lakebed in recent years.[17] Irrigation for agriculture represents the largest portion of consumptive water use in the watershed.

Humans have sculpted the lake's shorelines. In the early 1900s, federal action funded projects to build avian habitats by impounding wetlands, thus preventing some water from entering Great Salt Lake. The Bear River Migratory Bird Refuge[18] and the Farmington Bay Wildlife Management Area[19] were created during this time and are still notable refuges for resident and migrating birds (fig. 2).

Mineral extraction companies added diked evaporation ponds along the lake's edges (fig. 2). The ponds concentrate minerals from the salt water, such as sodium chloride (salt), potassium sulfate (potash for fertilizer), and magnesium chloride (metal used in steel and aluminum cans).[20] Since the companies use evaporation, this process also removes water from the system. Other industry on the lake includes the harvesting of brine shrimp cysts, which involves boats on the lake collecting the product, but processing does not consume water.[21]

Figure 2. An augmented Great Salt Lake. Black lines show constructed causeways, one for the railroad across the middle of the lake and the other for transportation to Antelope Island. The red structures are mineral extraction ponds, while the yellow areas are waterfowl impoundments. Illustration by Sheila A. Homburger.

Perhaps the most impactful intervention in the natural Great Salt Lake system was the building of a rock-filled railroad causeway across the middle of this enormous body of water in 1960 (fig. 2), creating a divided lake with two very different ecosystems.[22] The causeway cut off the north arm, Gunnison Bay, from river inputs, and the breach opening and culverts were too small to allow water to flow effectively between the north and south. As a result, the north arm water has become too saline (25 percent salt and higher) for brine shrimp, brine flies, or their microbial food to thrive.[23] Recent updates to the causeway in response to failing infrastructure created an expanded breach in 2016 and an opportunity to study exchange between the two arms,[24] as well as to investigate the potential for intervention to control salinity in the south arm of the lake.[25] After Great Salt Lake hit a historic low at the end of 2022, the state of Utah installed an adjustable rock berm in an effort to seal the breach and prevent the dense north arm water from flowing into the south arm. When the lake level rises, the water can spill over the berm, but in essence this alteration seals off the north arm from the south in a sacrificial gesture to support the south arm food chains.[26] In this altered ecosystem, the inflow of water, salt, and nutrients should be monitored with each change to record impacts on the biology.[27]

Human impacts have certainly limited the amount of water that enters Great Salt Lake, causing a rapid decline in lake elevation over the last two decades, with a 2022 record set for a historic low: 4,188.6 feet (1276.7 meters).[28] Following more than a century of diversions and interventions in the lake and its watershed, we are now experiencing the effects of anthropogenic climate change[29] and a mega-drought in the southwestern United States.[30] These conditions are predicted to cause warmer temperatures, more precipitation falling as rain instead of snow, and enhanced evaporation, putting additional pressure on an already taxed system.

Human impacts have made the habitat too dry and too salty, which threatens the biology of the lake. These changes will be felt by the microbes, the brine flies and shrimp, the millions of birds, and the humans that depend on and enjoy this ecosystem. The north arm unintentional "experiment" that cut off part of the lake from water inflows informs our actions today as the south arm gets saltier. We can look to the north arm of the lake to anticipate what may happen to the robust ecosystem of the south arm if the lake elevation continues to fall and salinity thus rises.

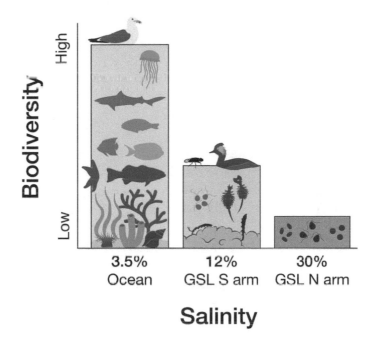

Figure 3. Biodiversity and food chain complexity decrease as salinity increases in saline systems. The ocean, at around 3.5 percent salts, is rich in biodiversity, whereas this is limited in the more saline south and north arms of Great Salt Lake. The food chains that birds depend on exist in the south arm and surrounding wetlands. Illustration by Sheila A. Homburger.

LIFE AND ENERGY IN THE DYNAMIC GREAT SALT LAKE

A diverse array of organisms have evolved to thrive in saline lakes.[31] From single-cell bacteria to small invertebrate animals, these saline life forms have secrets and strategies to manage the high salt content. Salt lakes around the world support a trophic structure with food chains and webs that vary based on the salinity and the type of salts present.[32] Great Salt Lake, due to its shallow lakebed, causeway, wetlands, and impoundments, features a salinity gradient from brackish (2–3 percent salts) to salt saturation (25–34 percent salts). This text focuses on the vibrant ecosystem centered in the south arm, Gilbert Bay, which has vacillated over time from a low salinity of 9 percent (1986) to a high salinity of 19 percent (2022).

Great Salt Lake is full of life, but the salinity level constrains the biodiversity. The less saline oceans, at around 3.5 percent salts, are teeming with diverse animal life and a rich array of primary producers supporting complicated food webs (fig. 3, left bar). The south arm of Great Salt Lake is limited, by salt concentrations higher than the ocean, to the simple shrimp and fly based food chains (fig. 3, center bar). Biodiversity in very salty water, such as the north arm, is further reduced, and the food chains disappear. Due to human impacts, the water in this extreme part of the lake exceeds 30 percent salinity in the summer and no longer supports invertebrates or the birds who eat them (fig. 3, right bar).[33] Microorganisms such as archaea, bacteria, and fungi are abundant but do not serve as food for consumers.[34] Thus, salinity is inversely correlated with biodiversity and food chain complexity.

The south arm of Great Salt Lake supports two slightly overlapping food chains: the benthic on the bottom of the lake and the pelagic in the water column. These are best visualized in a simple conceptual food chain model (fig. 4), which shows directional energy flow between the organisms at each trophic level.[35] At the foundational level of an aquatic ecosystem, primary producers do photosynthesis, capturing solar energy, thereby fueling the primary consumers who eat them. In Great Salt Lake, algae swimming in the water primarily feed brine shrimp, and cyanobacteria-based mats feed brine flies. A simple energy flow diagram shows birds as secondary consumers at Great Salt Lake, who eat the primary consumers (fig. 4). Other microorganisms may not be food but instead are involved in processing inputs and decomposing organic matter to release nutrients back into the ecosystem.[36]

While the relationships in more complex ecosystems are better modeled using food "webs," this approach is too intricate for the more limited interactions in Great Salt Lake. The saline water constrains the system (fig. 3), and the simple trophic conceptual food "chains" may serve to best illustrate the interactions in here.

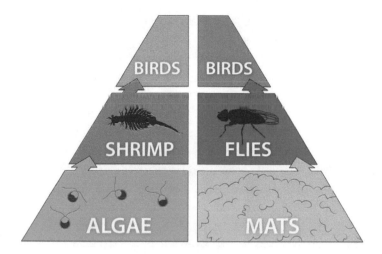

Figure 4. A simple conceptual food chain model for Great Salt Lake, showing trophic levels and directional energy flow. Note the primary producers on the bottom are represented by a larger area since their biomass and number should exceed that of the primary consumers in the middle. On the left is the pelagic brine shrimp centered food chain, while on the right is the benthic one centered on brine flies. Illustration by Sheila A. Homburger.

The linear nature and the pyramid shape point to a strong dependency on the primary producers (fig. 4), the loss of which would result in a collapse of the entire ecosystem.[37]

The secondary consumers at Great Salt Lake are birds. While some birds eat in the wetlands that surround the lake, here we will consider only those that feed from the open water. For the large number of species that depend on the south arm, two invertebrates sustain them: the brine shrimp (*Artemia franciscana*) in the water column,[38] and the brine flies (*Ephydra* species), which live in the benthic zone during their larval and pupal stages.[39] Some birds rely on both shrimp and flies, while others prefer one or the other. The *Artemia* and *Ephydra* are primary consumers who rely on large populations of primary producers, including algae and cyanobacteria associated with both the water column[40] and the microbialite structures on the bottom of the lake.[41] However, there is a small amount of crossover in these food chains: shrimp in the shallows may dine on the microbialites, and fly larvae floating the pelagic zone may eat the microalgae in the brine.[42]

The simple food chains in the south arm of Great Salt Lake are consistent in hypersaline lakes around the world that share similar biology, including brine shrimp, brine flies, and certain algae species.[43] Specific organisms associate with particular water chemistry across many salt lakes.[44] Significantly, nutrients (such as nitrogen and phosphorous) are abundant in hypersaline lakes, and primary productivity by photosynthesizers is relatively high.[45] Salinity is a driver, and there is a narrow range that is optimal for the ecosystem of a saline lake.[46] Too dilute, and other invertebrates may invade and become predators for the keystone shrimp and flies.[47] Too saline, and the animals are restricted from the microbial soup.[48]

How does biology flourish in Great Salt Lake under fluctuating salt conditions? Microorganisms, invertebrates, and birds that have evolved to live in salty brine have cellular strategies to regulate osmosis (fig. 5), which involve balancing the substances dissolved in the water outside the cell membrane with those on the inside of the cell by the movement of water. Salinity gradients also show distinct assemblages of life: the higher the salinity, the more stress the biology must overcome. At salt-saturation, such as in the north arm of Great Salt Lake, cells accumulate lipids or sugars inside to protect against water rushing out and shriveling the cells (fig. 5, right panel).[49] Even complex animals have means of getting rid of salt in their systems, which I discuss later in this text. In all life forms, these osmoregulation strategies are costly because they require energy to maintain.

Salty life forms each have a minimum, optimal, and maximum salinity range based on their strategies for overcoming salinity stress.[50] Osmotic adaptations, such as accumulating molecules inside (fig 5.), are common in both microorganisms and animals in places like Great Salt Lake. In general, managing higher salinity takes more of an organism's energy, leaving less energy for growth and reproduction. A recent report reviewing salinity impacts on Great Salt Lake suggests that above 15 percent total salts, the biology begins to

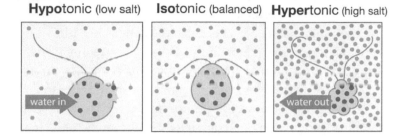

Figure 5. A model of osmoregulation in Great Salt Lake. The alga cell in the center is balanced in isotonic lake water of the south arm, where the salts on the outside of the cell (orange) balance the molecules that accumulate inside the cell (purple). For algae that have evolved to live in moderately salty brine, placing them in fresh or hypotonic water could cause them to lyse due to osmosis, as water would rush into the cell (*left*). In contrast, in hypertonic water such as the north arm, some algae may not be able to accumulate enough molecules to balance and osmosis would move water out, shriveling the cell (*right*). Illustration by Sheila A. Homburger.

struggle.[51] The decline in lake elevation in recent years is detrimental to the biology in part because of habitat loss, but mostly because of the salinity stress from increased concentration of salts.

Another concern in saline lake food chains is biomagnification of pollutants. In a terminal lake, water leaves through evaporation but other chemicals remain, so toxins accumulate. Research on Great Salt Lake has shown heavy metals in the water and lakebed, and they can be concentrated up the levels of the food chain. Mercury, for example, can be changed into an organic form by microorganisms in the benthic zone,[52] allowing the metal to accumulate in the tissues of the lake's animals.[53] This methyl mercury can even move from the lake into spiders on the land.[54] Likewise, selenium can enter animal systems.[55] Although mercury and selenium enter the lake as biproducts of mining, arsenic enters naturally from the surrounding mountain landscape, and it can also be concentrated up the food chains.[56]

This text focuses on the open water of the south arm, but some noteworthy interactions take place in other areas of the lake. The wetlands surrounding Great Salt Lake support less-saline and more-complex food webs.[57] Some shorebirds feed exclusively in these areas on more diverse invertebrates,[58] and others may use the area for nesting habitat.[59] In contrast, the hypersaline pink waters of the north arm, like other similar pink lake systems around the world, have no animal life but prevalent bacterial pseudo-photosynthesis capturing energy from light in addition to some high-salt algae species doing photosynthesis.[60] This salt-loving "halophile" population[61] is controlled by tiny predators: viruses that infect these microbes.[62] Though the north arm water does not support the vibrant food chains of Great Salt Lake, it does provide a significant isolated nesting location for American White Pelicans on Gunnison Island.[63] The biology of the entire lake ecosystem is thus more intricate and complex than the two open water food chains in the south arm.[64]

THE PELAGIC FOOD CHAIN

In aquatic biology, the term "pelagic" pertains to the water column of the open lake, which is distinct from the lake bottom, or benthic zone. The pelagic waters of the Great Salt Lake south arm are teeming with a diverse community of single-celled microalgae—the primary food source for the filter-feeding *Artemia* (fig. 6).[65] Algal abundance is impacted by salinity, seasonal temperature variation, and, of course, grazing by the shrimp.[66] Brine shrimp prefer some species, such as *Dunaliella viridis*. They have difficulty ingesting other microalgae, such as large diatoms, especially when shrimp are in their small juvenile stage.[67] Since they are filter feeders, *Artemia* may also eat smaller microorganisms.[68] Bacteria and archaea may associate with brine shrimp not only as food, but also as normal gut flora serving a probiotic, protective role.[69]

The life cycle of *Artemia franciscana* involves two interrelated pathways, one where the adults have live birth and one where they produce encysted embryos (cysts), in response to stressful conditions such as the onset of seasonal cold temperatures (fig. 7).[70] The cysts go into a state of reversable dormancy called diapause, and

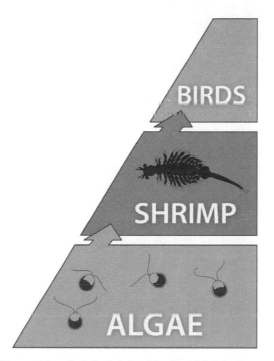

Figure 6. The pelagic food chain of the Great Salt Lake open water. Microalgae are the main primary producers, and brine shrimp are the primary consumers. A variety of bird species depend on the shrimp. Illustration by Sheila A. Homburger.

after months they enter quiescence that prepares them to hatch when the spring temperatures warm the lake water. As cysts, brine shrimp can endure periods of extreme conditions; their production is stimulated by low temperature, high salinity, or low oxygen stress.[71] These cysts are buoyant and float on the water, and they are collected as an industrial resource to be sold as feed for aquaculture of fish and prawns.[72]

The brine shrimp has the most efficient osmoregulatory system of any animal and tolerates large salinity and temperature ranges.[73] *Artemia* can reproduce well in the range of between 9 percent and 16 percent salts, with around 12 percent being optimum.[74] The osmolarity of their body fluids varies little with external

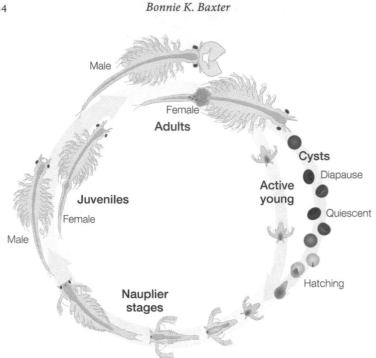

Figure 7. The life cycle of *Artemia franciscana*. Brine shrimp have live young, nauplii, that go through several life stages before becoming breeding adults. During stress, they shift their reproduction to encysted embryos, a dormant phase that survives winter or other adverse environmental conditions. Illustration by Sheila A. Homburger.

conditions.[75] In Great Salt Lake, salt ingested by shrimp through its food must be managed with special osmoregulation strategies.[76] One important feature is the shrimp's open circulatory system, which is in direct contact with their tissues. Hemolymph is the fluid that circulates in the cavity; it not only transports the salt ions, but it also accumulates organic molecules that help balance the fluid with the salts in the water the animal swims through (fig. 5). Brine shrimp have ion pumps that send salt out to regulate the salt composition of the hemolymph fluid, keeping it less saline than the gut fluid that is excreted.[77] In the nauplii stage (fig. 7), shrimp have a salt-expelling larval salt gland; this organ is absent in the adult shrimp.[78] Even the *Artemia* cysts possess a salt-balancing strategy: they accumulate the sugar trehalose to protect the embryo from shriveling.[79]

How is the pelagic food chain impacted as the water gets saltier? In the lab, brine shrimp's favorite algae food, *Dunaliella viridis*, grows more slowly as the salinity increases; their optimum salt concentration is similar to that of the shrimp that eat them.[80] Higher salinity thus means less food for the brine shrimp.[81] However, it is more complicated than that because some microalgal species may do better and some worse as the salt concentrations increase, and the nutrition of the *Artemia* will depend on the species available.[82] Also, with increasing salinity, the nutritional requirements and food foraging behavior for brine shrimp change.[83] Thus, brine shrimp reproduction rates are related to food source *quality* as well as *quantity*.

In addition to food scarcity, the shrimp themselves experience physiologic limitations with higher salinity.[84] All the strategies that allow *Artemia* to live in salty brine are costly, and the higher the salinity, the more energy they must put towards osmoregulation and away from other metabolisms. As a result, salinity beyond their optimal range limits growth, rates of development, reproduction, and survival. Adult *Artemia* will not reach full size in these conditions. This salinity stress response changes which genes are turned on or off in both adults and nauplii.[85] Above 15 percent salt, their genetic assembly lines for the stress pathways are in full production mode. The combined stressors of osmoregulation cost and food scarcity will shift *Artemia* reproduction towards cyst production instead of live birth (fig. 7).[86] Hypersaline waters can hold less oxygen, which causes additional stress for life in Great Salt Lake. As the salt concertation increases, there is less available oxygen, and the shrimp consume less.[87] However, *Artemia* can raise the level of pigments (analogous to hemoglobin) in their hemolymph to compensate, optimizing oxygen metabolism.[88]

In addition to salinity, temperature changes can affect *Artemia* in Great Salt Lake. The temperature we typically set our thermostats to in our homes, around 22°C, is optimal for brine shrimp

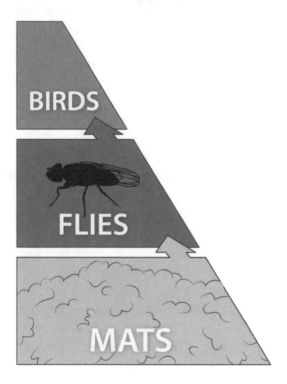

Figure 8. The benthic food chain of Great Salt Lake. Microbialite
mats contain the primary producers, and brine flies are the
primary consumers. A variety of bird species consume the flies.
Illustration by Sheila A. Homburger.

reproduction.[89] A shrinking, shallow lake may get warmer, in which
case both life span and reproduction rate will decrease significantly
for shrimp. Therefore, we must consider specific temperature/salinity
combinations when we think about optimal lake conditions for
Artemia.[90]

Brine shrimp can thrive at lower salt concentrations (e.g., 9–11
percent), but these conditions are outside their optimum range.
These salinities do not challenge brine shrimp physiology; rather,
they allow their predators, such as corixids or "water boatmen," to
thrive. With an exceptionally large influx of run-off in the 1980s,
the salinity of Great Salt Lake plummeted. Researchers measured

a multi-year decline in *Artemia* and observed a correlated increase in water boatman insects.[91] While much of the focus currently is on the dangers of a too-high salinity in the Great Salt Lake ecosystem, we should also note that problems arise when salinity falls too low. Managing an optimal salinity range in Great Salt Lake is critical for brine shrimp and thus for the entire pelagic ecosystem.

THE BENTHIC FOOD CHAIN

Beneath the open-water ecosystem is the benthic zone, the bottom of Great Salt Lake where the oxygen and sunlight are limited. The benthic food chain (fig. 8) features microbialite mats held together by a biofilm.[92] These mats provide both food and habitat for brine flies because the larvae eat the mats then pupate on their surface.[93] This simple food chain is complicated by the fact that flies in various stages of their life cycle feed distinct species of birds.

Microbialites are where biology meets geology. They are a complex mat of microorganisms, the actions of which, much like coral, cause calcium carbonate to precipitate out of the water, forming a rock that supports the mat.[94] In Great Salt Lake, these tire-sized mounds harness the sun's energy on the lake bottom. But since photosynthesis requires light, we find microbialites around the edges of the lake in the shallows where the sunlight can be absorbed, and this makes them very vulnerable to exposure when the lake elevation falls. The primary producers in the mats are cyanobacteria (e.g., *Euhalothece*) and diatoms (e.g., *Navicula*).[95] Cyanobacteria protect the mats and hold them together by secreting a polysaccharide (complex sugar) mucous layer. This biofilm also adheres the mat to the microbialite and helps collect precipitating minerals, which allows the mound to grow.

The brine flies depend on microbialite structures for much of their life cycle (fig. 9). The adult flies lay their eggs on the surface of the open water. The larvae hatch into the salty brine and wiggle their way to the bottom of the lake where they dine on the mats and grow. These flies live most of their life cycle in the water and

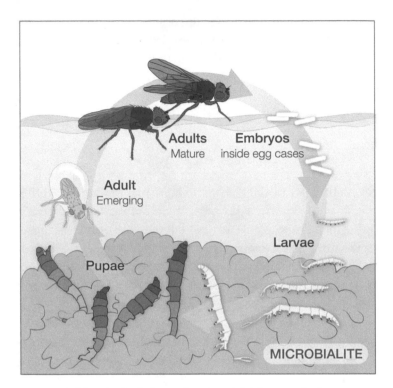

Figure 9. The life cycle of *Ephydra gracilis* at Great Salt Lake. Brine flies lay eggs on the lake surface, and these eggs hatch into larvae, which have three instar stages of growth. The larvae attach to the microbialites, which serve as both food and substrate, and they pupate. When the pupae hatch, the adult fly is born under water in an air bubble, which floats to the surface. Illustration by Sheila A. Homburger.

can overwinter as larvae over several months.[96] The microbialites are not only food, but also a substrate for pupation as the larvae attach and form a tiny cocoon on the bottom of the lake. The adult flies are born under water into an air bubble, which floats to the surface. The adults live only a few days, enough time to reproduce and perhaps feed some birds.

The family Ephydridae encompasses both shore and brine flies, and a few species inhabit the Great Salt Lake ecosystem.[97] In the open water of the south arm, we primarily find *Ephydra gracilis* while *Ephydra hians* prefers the wetland brackish water habitats where the salinity is lower. A shrinking, more-saline Great Salt Lake affects both the brine fly survival and also which species are present.

As evidenced in the dearth of flies and dead microbialites at the north arm of the lake, elevated salinity impacts the benthic food chain at each trophic level. Though both the cyanobacteria and the diatoms are flexible in fluctuating salinity, they have limits.[98] In laboratory experiments, when salt is above 15 percent, the mats die and detach from the rocky structure.[99] Recent field studies corroborate this phenomenon: microbialites around the lake in saltier water have thinner, dying mats, while near fresh groundwater seeps thicker mats persist. The other threat for microbialites is the shrinking shorelines as the exposed mats dry out and die when these structures in the shallows become exposed.[100]

Of course, if the microbialites are imperiled, brine fly larvae will have limited food, and if the structures are beached and dead, the flies will have no substrate on which to pupate. In California salt ponds that were above 14 percent salinity, *Ephydra gracilis* was smaller in size and had reduced hatching rates.[101] As with the brine shrimp, high salt may cause both food shortages and stress on the insects themselves. The increased energy requirements for the flies' osmoregulation in hypersaline waters has been shown to reduce growth and reproduction.[102] Also, because higher-saline water is denser, buoyancy makes it harder for Great Salt Lake brine fly larvae to descend through the water to their food.[103] Other parameters beyond salinity may impact *Ephydra* populations, such as nutrients, geochemistry, and temperature.[104]

In the ecology of Great Salt Lake, the benthic zone supports brine flies. *Ephydra* are keystone species, and their larvae, pupae, and adults feed countless birds.[105] Because of the economic inputs from the brine shrimp industry, management of the lake's biology has historically focused on *Artemia*.[106] But in the interest of a healthy ecosystem, researchers and managers should also be concerned about salinity impacts in the benthic zones that support the brine fly life cycle.

Birds: The Top of the Food Chains

Great Salt Lake is a critical stop on both the Central and Pacific Flyways for approximately ten million avian individuals, composed of more than three hundred species.[107] In addition to the birds on the open water, here we find one of the largest concentrations of shorebirds on Earth.[108] Birds are at the top of this food pyramid (fig. 4), and food scarcity is a concern. When salinity rises, birds that rely on *Artemia* and *Ephydra* may have limited, and less nutritious, food.[109] The excess salt also impacts waterbird physiology. How will birds, the secondary consumers of the food chains, respond to an ecosystem under stress?

First, let's explore which birds eat what. Some birds at Great Salt Lake are among the world's greatest distance migrants, and their mission at the lake, to feed and fatten and/or to nest, is met by the diversity of habitats including the wetlands. Food scarcity is a threat to their livelihood. Species that rely heavily on the south arm ecosystem may eat brine flies or shrimp at various stages of their life cycle (fig. 10).[110] Some birds may eat both, while others, such as the Phalarope species or Northern Shovelers, eat only one.

The ecosystem is more complicated than that, of course, especially considering the life cycles of the birds. For example, Green-winged Teal and Northern Shovelers rely on the lake's surrounding wetlands during migration and only heavily rely on shrimp in the winter when these fresher waters freeze.[111] Also, during breeding season, Wilson's Phalaropes feed in the wetlands on fresh or brackish invertebrates.[112]

Salinity impacts on invertebrates may cause birds to change where and what they eat, but they also will experience their own cost of osmoregulation. Birds in saline systems have evolved traits that help them cope with salt they ingest with their food to an extent.[113] Birds take in salt along with shrimp or fly larvae or pupae in the brine, and the bird must dispense with the excess. Some water birds have strategies to remove salt, such as salt glands that concentrate the mineral and excrete it through the nostrils (fig. 11).[114] When the water salinity is higher, water conservation becomes

Bird Species	Primary Food
Northern Shoveler	Brine shrimp (cysts, adults)
Green-Winged Teal	Brine shrimp (cysts)
Eared Grebe	Brine flies (adults, larvae) & Brine shrimp
California Gull	Brine flies (adults) & Brine shrimp
Red-Necked & Wilson's Phalarope	Brine flies (all life stages)
Common Goldeneye	Brine flies (larvae, pupae)

Figure 10. The diet of birds that depend on the south arm and are in high population numbers at Great Salt Lake. Illustration by Sheila A. Homburger.

more critical, and the excess electrolytes are energetically taxing on their organs. Avian kidneys have a limited ability to concentrate and remove salts.[115] Also, salt can accumulate in the digestive system, and birds can lose water through respiration and evaporation through their skin.[116] Since high salinity can cause birds to overspend their energy budget, these conditions may result in a reduced

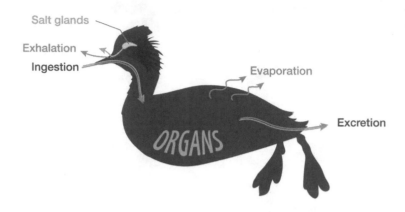

Figure 11. Salt accumulation and water loss in water birds. Osmoregulation strategies are energetically taxing if the brine becomes too salty. Under such conditions, the path of salt is shown in gold and that of water in blue. Excess salt is ingested when eating invertebrates from the hypersaline water. The salt may concentrate in the salt glands, and some of it will be expelled later from the nostrils. Salt may also be excreted in the bird's waste or accumulate in organs such as the kidneys. Water loss is also impactful to birds as they can become dehydrated. Water can be lost through respiration when they exhale, evaporation through the skin, and excrement. Illustration by Sheila A. Homburger.

immune response,[117] loss of body weight,[118] or reduced feather insulation.[119]

Thus, osmoregulation stress may affect bird populations directly, not just indirectly through food scarcity. Other direct impacts for some species may be more frequent trips to freshwater, increased travel to find food, or loss of nesting habitat. Not only could a shrinking lake make the open water and wetland ponds too salty, but salinity changes may also reduce the plant cover for nesting around the shores. Management strategies for saline bird habitats should seek an optimal salinity range to protect water birds; indirect measures, such as assessing the invertebrate population on which they feed, are not enough.[120] Scoring both direct and indirect impacts may inform the process and lead to a better target range goal.

The significance of the Great Salt Lake system for birds cannot be overstated. Some birds may nest and rear young at the lake, while other avian migrators may stop over to power long flights. Foraging behavior and diet can differ over life stages or seasons and factors such as water depth, vegetation, and food type may fluctuate for a given species. All these options are available at this one location. Great Salt Lake is such an asset for birds, notably for its large size, but more importantly for the unique diversity of habitats it provides.

FLEXIBILITY, REFUGIA, AND RESILIENCY

The food chains of Great Salt Lake are certainly stressed during periods of low elevation and concomitant high salinity. But this biological system has evolved to tolerate the fluctuating conditions typical of a terminal lake, and each life form has its own strategies for surviving tough times. Some employ simple strategies, such as food switching for birds or invertebrates, or more complex responses involving switching genes on and off. The Great Salt Lake ecosystem is flexible and resilient. But it is also fragile if the stressor goes on for too long, as observed in the decades-long sequestration of the lake's north arm, which limited life to the microbial realm (fig. 3, right bar). As terminal lakes shrink and swell, and salinity vacillates, what are the vulnerabilities? Given climate change pressures, this is an urgent question.[121]

At the bottom of the food chains, the primary producers must manage to reproduce in large numbers and complete the biochemistry of photosynthesis. High salinity conditions slow metabolism and growth rates for microalgae such as *Dunaliella viridis*,[122] which lowers the food supply for brine shrimp. Since this algal species can accumulate glycerol inside to balance as the salt concentration increases, *Dunaliella* survives during times of cellular stress (fig. 12). And perhaps it provides more nutrition for the shrimp as it becomes a fatty food resource, even though it is scarce in number. Some microbial species may be able to survive in a slower growth state because competition from other algae and cyanobacteria, as well as predation by animals, is restricted by the high salt conditions. Microalgae may then rebound in population from their small resilient population when the lake water gets diluted with spring runoff.

In the Great Salt Lake benthic mats, the dominant producer is the cyanobacteria, *Euhalothece*.[123] Several features of this microbe allow it to survive osmoregulation stress, including ion pumps to remove salt and antioxidants that can prevent cellular damage.[124] However, the mats suffer additional stress from desiccation when the microbialite mounds are dried on the shoreline of the shrinking lake. Many cyanobacteria produce a sugary mucous coating, which sticks the microbes together in a biofilm and collects mineral grains from the water to form mounds in the benthic zone.[125] Protection from dehydration may be a secondary function of this mucous matrix, but it would most certainly aid in retaining moisture (fig. 12). Microbialites may also resist other climate change impacts beyond drought as mats have been shown to grow robustly in the face of changing carbon dioxide levels and acidification of the oceans.[126] Microbialite recovery has been reported in other systems,[127] and we have seen recolonization at Great Salt Lake when dried microbialites were returned to lake water, suggesting that over the timescale of months they are resilient.[128]

Because microorganisms like algae and cyanobacteria have rapid generation times and exist in large population numbers, they should be resilient in the face of short-term changes. However, it is important to note that microbialites in the north arm, where they have been at high salinity for decades, are vestiges, and the mats there have died.[129] Algal diversity is much lower at that site. It is unclear how long microbialite mats or algal communities can survive conditions that are too salty or too dry and still recover. If the lake level rises significantly in the future, the flexibility of microorganisms may help the ecosystem rebound before it reaches an ecological tipping point.

Brine shrimp may be one of the most flexible animals on our planet.[130] The ability of *Artemia* to osmoregulate under a huge salinity range, from 2 percent to more than 30 percent, explains their success in such extreme environments. Also, as filter feeders, shrimp are omnivores limited only by the size of their food, and their diet can flex based on food availability. Another strategy that the brine shrimp possess is the ability to switch their reproductive mode from live birth to encysted embryos when conditions are stressful, and the cyoto can remain dormant until favorable conditions return (fig. 12). The *Artemia* industry leverages this reproductive flexibility, planning cyst harvests for the late fall when temperatures drop in the lake water and the cysts are abundant.[131] Brine shrimp cysts that are dehydrated are stable over decades, which is another important strategy for managing life in a lake that could become a dry lakebed, then refill, vacillating over time. During cyst production, the embryos produce protective molecules that help them resist desiccation and other adverse situations.[132] When in their encysted form, they can withstand harsh conditions that would kill the adult *Artemia*—even high pressure, microgravity, and other extremes that would allow them to survive in outer space![133]

Brine flies are less flexible than the shrimp, as their reproduction rates are more sensitive to elevated salinity.[134] They do accumulate osmotically balancing molecules inside their bodies and pump salt out, but the *Ephydra* are not adept above a certain threshold.[135] Their saving grace is the mobility of the winged adult flies, which allows them to lay their eggs outside of the south arm bays and in small groundwater ponds and seeps on the lake margins. If the lake is too salty, they can survive in the wetlands and wait to repopulate the lake when the elevation recovers, and salinity is lower. These "refugia" pools provide a place for fly larvae and pupae to continue the life cycle (fig. 12). Such safe havens may protect the biodiversity of the Great Salt Lake system, especially the invertebrates, as climate change effects escalate.[136] For example, if the lake habitat is disturbed or lost, the refugia serve an especially crucial role.[137] Identifying and protecting these places should be a priority for lake management and conservation.

At each trophic level, the life of Great Salt Lake has a method to manage during times when the salinity is elevated and the lake shore recessed (fig. 12). These combined biological strategies for

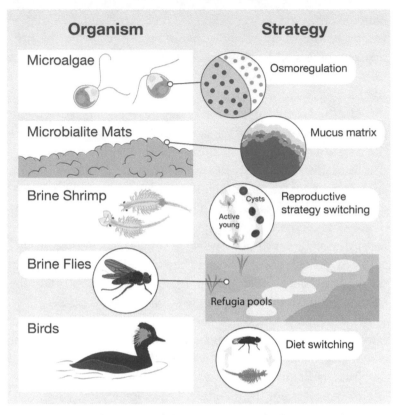

Figure 12. Strategies of resiliency. Life forms in Great Salt Lake all possess mechanisms to survive short periods of elevated salinity and drying. Illustration by Sheila A. Homburger.

flexibility and resiliency can override the fragility of a system that is balanced on only two keystone invertebrates. Future studies, however, should explore how long the system can endure under stress. The Great Salt Lake north arm "experiment" (begun in 1960), where the saturated salt water restricts so many life forms, suggests that decades of these conditions may exhaust the limits of the system's flexibility. The timeline of stress and recovery are important to consider.

A focus on delivering more water to Great Salt Lake is in line with calls for conservation in the watersheds of other saline lakes in a similar water crisis.[138] The obstacles that challenge possible

solutions are not only pressures from climate change, but also exist-
ing water rights, laws, and policies. A single approach, like a single
arrow, will not solve the water crisis; it will require a quiver of
arrows. Recent policy changes in Utah[139] and work on identifying
paths for success[140] bring optimism.

If we can let more water flow to the lake, the biology will rebound.
Indeed, the heavy winter snow of 2023 produced the first elevation
bump in more than a decade, giving life in the lake a short reprieve.
The food chains of Great Salt Lake are wired for success in a fluctuating system that challenges the very existence of life.

NOTES

1. Western Hemisphere Shorebird Reserve Network, "Great Salt Lake:
   Celebrating 30 Years as a WHSRN Site," https://whsrn.org/great-salt-
   lake-celebrating-30-years/; Doyle W. Stephens, "Changes in lake levels,
   salinity and the biological community of Great Salt Lake (Utah, USA),
   1847–1987," *Hydrobiologia* 197 (1990): 139–46.
2. Ella Dibble Sorensen, Heidi Morrill Hoven, and John Neill, "Great Salt
   Lake Shorebirds, Their Habitats, and Food Base," in *Great Salt Lake
   Biology: A Terminal Lake in a Time of Change*, ed. Bonnie K. Baxter and
   Jaimi K. Butler (Springer, Cham, 2020), 263–309.
3. Mattia Saccò et al., "Salt To Conserve: A Review on the Ecology and
   Preservation of Hypersaline Ecosystems," *Biological Reviews* 96, no. 6
   (2021): 2828–50.
4. United States Geologic Survey, Great Salt Lake Hydromapper, https://
   webapps.usgs.gov/gsl/index.html, accessed November 2, 2023.
5. Robert E. Cohenour and K. C. Thompson, "Geologic Setting of Great Salt
   Lake," *The Great Salt Lake*, Utah Geological Association, Salt Lake City:
   (1966): 35–56.
6. Genevieve Atwood, Tammy J. Wambeam, and N. John Anderson, "The
   Present as a Key to the Past: Paleoshoreline Correlation Insights from
   Great Salt Lake," in *Lake Bonneville: A Scientific Update*, ed. Charles G.
   Oviatt and John F. Shroder (Elsevier, 2016), 1–27.
7. John F. Shroder et al., "Landslides, Alluvial Fans, and Dam Failure at Red
   Rock Pass: The Outlet of Lake Bonneville," in *Lake Bonneville: A Scientific
   Update*, ed. Charles G. Oviatt and John F. Shroder (Elsevier, 2016), 75–87.
8. Charles G. Oviatt et al., "Reinterpretation of the Burmester Core,
   Bonneville Basin, Utah," *Quaternary Research* 52, no. 2 (1999): 180–84.
9. Atwood, Wambeam, and Anderson, "Paleoshoreline Correlation," 1–27;
   Shroder et al., "Red Rock Pass," 75–87.

10.   D. B. Madsen, "The Early Human Occupation of the Bonneville Basin," in
      Lake Bonneville: A Scientific Update, ed. Charles G. Oviatt and John F.
      Shroder (Elsevier, 2016) 504–25; David B. Madsen, "Environmental
      Change during the Pleistocene-Holocene Transition and Its Possible
      Impact on Human Populations," in Models for the Millennium: Great
      Basin Anthropology Today, ed. Charlotte Beck (Salt Lake City: University
      of Utah Press, 1999), 75–82.
11.   Stuart J. Baldwin, "Archaeological Salt at Mesa Verde and Trade with
      Areas to the North and West," Kiva 42, no. 2 (1976): 177–91.
12.   Forrest S. Cuch, History of Utah's American Indians (Denver: University
      Press of Colorado, 2000).
13.   John Charles Frémont, Report of the Exploring Expedition to the Rocky
      Mountains in the Year 1842: And to Oregon and North California in the
      Years 1843–44, Vol. 1 (Gales and Seaton, printers, 1845).
14.   Howard Stansbury, Exploration of the Valley of the Great Salt Lake:
      Including a Reconnaissance of a New Route through the Rocky Mountains
      (Philadelphia: Lippincott, Gramabo & Co., 1855).
15.   Bonnie K. Baxter, "Great Salt Lake Microbiology: A Historical Perspec-
      tive," International Microbiology 21, no. 3 (2018): 79–95.
16.   Sarah E. Null and Wayne A. Wurtsbaugh, "Water Development,
      Consumptive Water Uses, and Great Salt Lake," in Great Salt Lake
      Biology: A Terminal Lake in a Time of Change, ed. Bonnie K. Baxter and
      Jaimi K. Butler (Springer, Cham, 2020), 1–21.
17.   Wayne A. Wurtsbaugh et al., "Decline of the World's Saline
      Lakes," Nature Geoscience 10, no. 11 (2017): 816–21.
18.   C. S. Williams and W. H. Marshall, "Duck Nesting Studies, Bear River
      Migratory Bird Refuge, Utah, 1937," Journal of Wildlife Management
      (1938): 29–48; John B. Van Den Akker and Vanez T. Wilson, "Twenty
      Years of Bird Banding at Bear River Migratory Bird Refuge,
      Utah," Journal of Wildlife Management 13, no. 4 (1949): 359–76.
19.   Richard A. Jaynes and Reynold D. Willie, "Mapping of Wildlife Habitat in
      Farmington Bay, Utah," CRSC Report 82–1, NASA Center for Aerospace
      Information 1.26: 168975 (1982).
20.   Peter Behrens, "Industrial Processing of Great Salt Lake Brines by Great
      Salt Lake Minerals and Chemicals Corporation," in Great Salt Lake: A
      Scientific, Historical, and Economic Overview 116, ed. Wallace J. Gwynn
      (1980), 223; Thomas G. Tripp, "Production of Magnesium from Great Salt
      Lake, Utah USA," Natural Resources and Environmental Issues 15, no. 1
      (2009): 10.
21.   Brad Marden, Phil Brown, and Thomas Bosteels, "Great Salt Lake
      Artemia: Ecosystem Functions and Services with a Global Reach," in
      Great Salt Lake Biology: A Terminal Lake in a Time of Change, ed. Bonnie
      K. Baxter and Jaimi K. Butler (Springer, Cham, 2020), 175–237.

22. J. S. Cannon and M. A. Cannon, "The Southern Pacific Railroad Trestle, Past and Present," in *Great Salt Lake: An Overview of Change*, ed. J. Wallace Gwynn (Utah Geological Survey, 2002): 343–74.

23. Thomas C. Adams, "Salt Migration to the Northwest Body of Great Salt Lake, Utah," *Science* 143, no. 3610 (1964): 1027–29; Swati Almeida-Dalmet and Bonnie K. Baxter, "Unexpected Complexity at Salinity Saturation: Microbial Diversity of the North Arm of Great Salt Lake," in *Great Salt Lake Biology: A Terminal Lake in a Time of Change*, ed. Bonnie K. Baxter and Jaimi K. Butler (Springer, Cham, 2020), 119–44.

24. James S. White, Sarah E. Null, and David G. Tarboton, "How do Changes to the Railroad Causeway in Utah's Great Salt Lake Affect Water and Salt Flow?," *PLOS One* 10, no. 12 (2015): e0144111.

25. Phil D. Brown, Thomas Bosteels, and Brad T. Marden, "Salt Load Transfer and Changing Salinities across a New Causeway Breach in Great Salt Lake: Implications for Adaptive Management," *Lakes & Reservoirs: Research & Management* 28, no. 1 (2023): e12421.

26. Spencer J. Cox, "Gov, Cox Issues Executive Order to Raise the Great Salt Lake Causeway Berm," Utah.gov, https://governor.utah.gov/2023/02/03/gov-cox-issues-executive-order-to-raise-the-great-salt-lake-causeway-berm/, accessed November 2, 2023.

27. Ibrahim Nourein Mohammed and David G. Tarboton, "An Examination of the Sensitivity of the Great Salt Lake to Changes in Inputs," *Water Resources Research* 48, no. 11 (2012).

28. United States Geologic Survey, Great Salt Lake Hydromapper, accessed November 2, 2023.

29. Bonnie K. Baxter and Jaimi K. Butler, "Climate Change and Great Salt Lake," in *Great Salt Lake Biology: A Terminal Lake in a Time of Change*, ed. Bonnie K. Baxter and Jaimi K. Butler (Springer, Cham, 2020), 23–52.

30. A. Park Williams, Benjamin I. Cook, and Jason E. Smerdon, "Rapid Intensification of the Emerging Southwestern North American Mega-drought in 2020–2021," *Nature Climate Change* 12, no. 3 (2022): 232–34.

31. Saccò, "Review Ecology Hypersaline Ecosystems," 2828–50.

32. F. D. Por, "A Classification of Hypersaline Waters, Based on Trophic Criteria," *Marine Ecology* 1, no. 2 (1980): 121–31; N. V. Shadrin and E. V. Anufriieva, "Structure and Trophic Relations in Hypersaline Environments," *Biology Bulletin Reviews* 10 (2020): 48–56.

33. Almeida-Dalmet, "Microbial Diversity of the North Arm," 119–144.

34. Carlos Pedrós-Alió et al., "The Microbial Food Web along Salinity Gradients," *FEMS Microbiology Ecology* 32, no. 2 (2000): 143–155; Bonnie K. Baxter and Polona Zalar, "The Extremophiles of Great Salt Lake: Complex Microbiology in a Dynamic Hypersaline Ecosystem," in *Model Ecosystems in Extreme Environments*, ed. Joseph Seckbach and Pabulo H. Rampelotto (Elsevier, Netherlands, 2019), 57–99.

35.   Gerd-Joachim Krauss and Dietrich H. Nies, *Ecological Biochemistry: Environmental and Interspecies Interactions*, John Wiley & Sons, (2015).
36.   David Naftz et al., "Anthropogenic Influences on the Input and Biogeo-chemical Cycling of Nutrients and Mercury in Great Salt Lake, Utah, USA," *Applied Geochemistry* 23, no. 6 (2008): 1731–44; D. Naftz, "Inputs and Internal Cycling of Nitrogen to a Causeway Influenced, Hypersaline Lake, Great Salt Lake, Utah, USA," *Aquatic Geochemistry* 23, no. 3 (2017): 199–216.
37.   Melody R. Lindsay et al., "Effects of Salinity on Microbialite-Associated Production in Great Salt Lake, Utah," *Ecology* 100, no. 3 (2019): e02611.
38.   Marden, "Great Salt Lake *Artemia*," 175–237.
39.   N. Collins, "Population Ecology of *Ephydra cinerea* Jones (Diptera: Ephydridae), the Only Benthic Metazoan of the Great Salt Lake, USA," *Hydrobiologia* 68 (1980): 99–112.
40.   G. E. Belovsky et al., "The Great Salt Lake Ecosystem (Utah, USA): Long Term Data and a Structural Equation Approach," *Ecosphere* 2, no. 3 (2011): 1–40; Phil D. Brown et al., "DNA Metabarcoding of the Phyto-plankton of Great Salt Lake's Gilbert Bay: Spatiotemporal Assemblage Changes and Comparisons to Microscopy," *Journal of Great Lakes Research* 48, no. 1 (2022): 110–24.
41.   Melody R. Lindsay, Eric C. Dunham, and Eric S. Boyd, "Microbialites of Great Salt Lake," in *Great Salt Lake Biology: A Terminal Lake in a Time of Change*, ed. Bonnie K. Baxter and Jaimi K. Butler (Springer, Cham, 2020), 87–118.
42.   Katherine L. Barrett, "Microbialite Communities and Food Web Linkages in Great Salt Lake, Utah, USA" (PhD diss., University of Notre Dame, 2021), accessed November 2, 2023, https://www.proquest.com/openview/e5f8f8b9931ff3063914fd7246469cd9/1?pq-rigsite=gscholar&cbl=18750&diss=y; Katherine L. Barrett and Gary E. Belovsky, "Invertebrates and Phytoplankton of Great Salt Lake: Is Salinity the Driving Factor?," in *Great Salt Lake Biology: A Terminal Lake in a Time of Change*, ed. Bonnie K. Baxter and Jaimi K. Butler (Springer, Cham, 2020), 145–73.
43.   Por, "Hypersaline Trophic Criteria," 21–31.
44.   David B. Herbst, "Gradients of Salinity Stress, Environmental Stability and Water Chemistry as a Templet for Defining Habitat Types and Physiological Strategies in Inland Salt Waters," in *Saline Lakes: Publications from the 7th International Conference on Salt Lakes, held in Death Valley National Park, California, USA, September 1999* (Springer Netherlands, 2001), 209–19.
45.   Shadrin, "Trophic Relations Hypersaline Environments," 48–56.
46.   Senner et al., "A Salt Lake under Stress: Relationships among Birds, Water Levels, and Invertebrates at a Great Basin Saline Lake," *Biological Conservation* 220 (2018): 320–329.

47. Wayne A. Wurtsbaugh and Therese Smith Berry, "Cascading Effects of Decreased Salinity on the Plankton Chemistry, and Physics of the Great Salt Lake (Utah)," *Canadian Journal of Fisheries and Aquatic Sciences* 47, no. 1 (1990): 100–109.

48. Almeida-Dalmet, "Microbial Diversity of the North Arm," 119–44.

49   Salma Mukhtar, Malik Kauser Abdulla, and Mehnaz Samina, "Osmoadaptation in Halophilic Bacteria and Archaea," *Research Journal of Biotechnology* Vol 15 (2020): 5.

50. Pedrós-Alió, "Microbial Food Web," 143–55; Herbst, "Gradients of Salinity Stress," 209–19.

51. Great Salt Lake Salinity Advisory Committee, "Influence of Salinity on the Resources and Uses of Great Salt Lake," 2021, Utah Geological Survey Open File Report, Department of Natural Resources, https://doi. org/10.34191/OFR-736, accessed November 2, 2023.

52. Eric S. Boyd et al., "Effect of Salinity on Mercury Methylating Benthic Microbes and Their Activities in Great Salt Lake, Utah," *Science of the Total Environment* 581 (2017): 495–506.

53. Abigail F. Scott and Frank J. Black, "Mercury Bioaccumulation and Biomagnification in Great Salt Lake Ecosystems," in *Great Salt Lake Biology: A Terminal Lake in a Time of Change*, ed. Bonnie K. Baxter and Jaimi K. Butler (Springer, Cham, 2020), 435–461; Jacob Wright, Shu Yang, and William P. Johnson et al., "Temporal Correspondence of Selenium and Mercury among Brine Shrimp and Water in Great Salt Lake, Utah, USA," *Science of the Total Environment* 749 (2020): 141273.

54. Heidi J. Saxton et al., "Maternal Transfer of Inorganic Mercury and Methylmercury in Aquatic and Terrestrial Arthropods," *Environmental Toxicology and Chemistry* 32, no. 11 (2013): 2630–36.

55. Wayne A. Wurtsbaugh, "Biostromes, Brine Flies, Birds and the Bioaccumulation of Selenium in Great Salt Lake, Utah," *Natural Resources and Environmental Issues* 15, no. 1 (2009): 2; Wright, "Selenium and Mercury Great Salt Lake," 141273; William P. Johnson et al., "Conceptual Model for Selenium Cycling in the Great Salt Lake," *The Division of Water Quality of the Utah Department of Environmental Quality* (2006).

56. Kevin V. Brix, Rick D. Cardwell, and William J. Adams, "Chronic Toxicity of Arsenic to the Great Salt Lake Brine Shrimp, *Artemia franciscana*," *Ecotoxicology and Environmental Safety* 54, no. 2 (2003): 169–75.

57. David C. Richards et al., "Ecology and Food Web Dynamics of an Effluent Dominated Wetland, Great Salt Lake, UT," *Progress Report to North Davis Sewer District, OreoHelix Ecological, Vineyard, Utah* (2020); Brad Marden and David C. Richards, "Multi-Year Investigations of Complex Interactions between Cyanobacteria Blooms and the Food Web in Farmington Bay, Great Salt Lake, Utah: A Progress Report of Scientific Findings," *Wasatch Front Water Quality Council* (2019).

58. Sorensen, "Great Salt Lake Shorebirds," 263–309.
59. Michael R. Conover and Mark E. Bell, "Importance of Great Salt Lake to Pelagic Birds: Eared Grebes, Phalaropes, Gulls, Ducks, and White Pelicans," in *Great Salt Lake Biology: A Terminal Lake in a Time of Change*, ed. Bonnie K. Baxter and Jaimi K. Butler (Springer, Cham, 2020), 239–62.
60. Por, "Hypersaline Trophic Criteria," 121–31.
61. Almeida-Dalmet, "Microbial Diversity of the North Arm," 119–44.
62. Bonnie K. Baxter, Mihnea R. Mangalea, Smaranda Willcox et al., "Haloviruses of Great Salt Lake: a Model for Understanding Viral Diversity," in *Halophiles and Hypersaline Environments: Current Research and Future Trends,* ed. Antonio Ventosa, Aharon Oren, and Yanhe Ma (2011): 173–90.
63. Ashley M. Kijowski et al., "American White Pelicans of Gunnison Island, Great Salt Lake, Utah," in *Great Salt Lake Biology: A Terminal Lake in a Time of Change*, ed. Bonnie K. Baxter and Jaimi K. Butler (Springer, Cham, 2020), 311–44.
64. Barrett, "Invertebrates and Phytoplankton," 145–73.
65. Belovsky, "Great Salt Lake Ecosystem," 1–40; Marden, "Great Salt Lake *Artemia*," 175–237.
66. Marden, "Great Salt Lake *Artemia*," 175–237.
67. Doyle Stephens, "Salinity-Induced Changes in the Aquatic Ecosystem of Great Salt Lake, Utah," in *Utah Geological Association Guidebook 26*, ed. Janet K. Pitman and Alan R. Carroll, (1998): 1–8.
68. Liying Sui et al., "Archaea *Haloferax* Supplementation Improves *Artemia* Biomass Production in Hypersaline Conditions," *Aquaculture* 528 (2020): 735540.
69. Misty R. Riddle, Bonnie K. Baxter, and Brian J. Avery, "Molecular Identification of Microorganisms Associated with the Brine Shrimp *Artemia franciscana*," *Aquatic Biosystems* 9 (2013): 1–11; Laurent Verschuere et al., "Selected Bacterial Strains Protect *Artemia* spp. from the Pathogenic Effects of *Vibrio proteolyticus* CW8T2," *Applied and Environmental Microbiology* 66, no. 3 (2000): 1139–46.
70. Marden, "Great Salt Lake *Artemia*," 175–237.
71. Steven C. Hand, "Quiescence in *Artemia franciscana* Embryos: Reversible Arrest of Metabolism and Gene Expression at Low Oxygen Levels," *Journal of Experimental Biology* 201, no. 8 (1998): 1233–42.
72. Marden, "Great Salt Lake *Artemia*," 175–237.
73. P. C. Croghan, "The Osmotic and Ionic Regulation of *Artemia salina* (L.)," *Journal of Experimental Biology* 35, no. 1 (1958): 219–33.
74. George V. Triantaphyllidis et al., "International Study on *Artemia* XLIX. Salinity Effects on Survival, Maturity, Growth, Biometrics, Reproductive and Lifespan Characteristics of a Bisexual and a Parthenogenetic Population of *Artemia*," *Hydrobiologia* 302 (1995): 215–27.

75. F. P. Conte, G. L. Peterson, and R. D. Ewing, "Larval Salt Gland of *Artemia salina* nauplii: Regulation of Protein Synthesis by Environmental Salinity," *Journal of Comparative Physiology* 82 (1973): 277–89.
76. Croghan, "Osmotic Regulation in Artemia," 243–49.
77. Jehan-Hervé Lignot and Guy Charmantier, "Osmoregulation and Excretion," *Natural History of Crustacea* 4 (2015): 249–85; Stephanie De Vos et al., "The Genome of the Extremophile *Artemia* Provides Insight into Strategies to Cope with Extreme Environments," *BMC Genomics* 22, no. 1 (2021): 1–26.
78. Conte, "Larval Salt Gland *Artemia*," 277–89.
79. Thomas H. MacRae, "Molecular Chaperones, Stress Resistance and Development in *Artemia franciscana*," *Seminars in Cell & Developmental Biology*, vol. 14, no. 5, (2003): 251–258.
80. Duc Tran et al., "Identification of *Dunaliella viridis* Using Its Markers," *International Journal of Applied Science and Technology* 3, no. 4 (2013): 118–26.
81. Barrett, "Invertebrates and Phytoplankton," 145–73.
82. Fereidun Mohebbi, "The Brine Shrimp *Artemia* and Hypersaline Environments Microalgal Composition: a Mutual Interaction," *International Journal of Aquatic Science* 1, no. 1 (2010): 19–27.
83. John Davenport and Aine Healy, "Relationship between Medium Salinity, Body Density, Buoyancy and Swimming in *Artemia franciscana* Larvae: Constraints on Water Column Use?," *Hydrobiologia* 556 (2006): 295–301.
84. R. A. Browne and G. Wanigasekera, "Combined Effects of Salinity and Temperature on Survival and Reproduction of Five Species of *Artemia*," *Journal of Experimental Marine Biology and Ecology* 244, no. 1 (2000): 29–44; Gayle L. Dana and Petra H. Lenz, "Effects of Increasing Salinity on an *Artemia* Population from Mono Lake, California," *Oecologia* 68, no. 3 (1986): 428–36; Theodore J. Abatzopoulos et al., "Effects of Salinity and Temperature on Reproductive and Life Span Characteristics of Clonal *Artemia* (International Study on *Artemia* LXVI)," *Hydrobiologia* 492 (2003): 191–99.
85. Stephanie De Vos et al., "Identification of Salt Stress Response Genes Using the *Artemia* Transcriptome," Aquaculture 500, (February 2019): 305–14; JunMo Lee, Byung Cheol Cho, and Jong Soo Park, "Transcriptomic Analysis of Brine Shrimp *Artemia franciscana* across a Wide Range of Salinities," *Marine Genomics* 61 (2022): 100919.
86. Fereidun Mohebbi, "The Brine Shrimp *Artemia* and Hypersaline Environments Microalgal Composition: a Mutual Interaction," *International Journal of Aquatic Science* no. 1 (2010): 19–27; Abatzopoulos, "Reproductive and Life Span Characteristics *Artemia*," 191–99.
87. Sandra Irwin, Vanessa Wall, and John Davenport, "Measurement of Temperature and Salinity Effects on Oxygen Consumption of *Artemia franciscana*, Measured Using Fibre-optic Oxygen Microsensors," *Hydrobiologia* 575 (2007): 109–15.

88. Barbara M. Gilchrist, "Haemoglobin in *Artemia*," *Proceedings of the Royal Society of London, Series B-Biological Sciences* 143, no. 910 (1954): 136–46.

89. Abatzopoulos, "Reproductive and Life Span Characteristics *Artemia*," 191–99.

90. Browne, "Salinity and Temperature *Artemia*," 29–44.

91. W. A. Wurtsbaugh, "Food-Web Modification by an Invertebrate Predator in the Great Salt Lake (USA)," *Oecologia* 89, no. 2 (1992): 168–75.

92. Stefan J. Green et al., "A Salinity and Sulfate Manipulation of Hypersaline Microbial Mats Reveals Stasis in the Cyanobacterial Community Structure," *ISME Journal* 2, no. 5 (2008): 457–70.

93. Collins, "Population Ecology of *Ephydra*," 99–112.

94. Lindsay, "Microbialites of Great Salt Lake," 87–118.

95. Melody R. Lindsay et al., "Microbialite Response to an Anthropogenic Salinity Gradient in Great Salt Lake, Utah," *Geobiology* 15, no. 1 (2017): 131–45.

96. Collins, "Population Ecology of *Ephydra*," 99–112.

97. Sabrina Haney, Oscar Bedolla, and Jonathan B. Clark, "DNA Barcodes for Great Salt Lake Brine Flies Establish a Baseline for Monitoring Changes in Biodiversity," *Inland Waters* 13, no. 1 (2023): 101–10.

98. Hee Wook Yang et al., "Genomic Survey of Salt Acclimation-Related Genes in the Halophilic Cyanobacterium *Euhalothece* sp. Z-M001," *Scientific Reports* 10, no. 1 (2020): 1–11; Vera Nikitashina, Daniel Stettin, and Georg Pohnert, "Metabolic Adaptation of Diatoms to Hypersalinity," *Phytochemistry* 201 (2022): 113267.

99. Lindsay, "Salinity Microbialite-Associated Production," e02611.

100. Frantz, Carie M. et al., "Desiccation of Ecosystem-Critical Microbialites in the Shrinking Great Salt Lake, Utah (USA)," *PLOS Water*, (2023): e000010.

101. David B. Herbst, "Salinity Controls on Trophic Interactions among Invertebrates and Algae of Solar Evaporation Ponds in the Mojave Desert and Relation to Shorebird Foraging and Selenium Risk," *Wetlands* 26, no. 2 (2006): 475–85.

102. David B. Herbst, "Developmental and Reproductive Costs of Osmoregulation to an Aquatic Insect that is a Key Food Resource to Shorebirds at Salt Lakes Threatened by Rising Salinity and Desiccation," *Frontiers in Ecology and Evolution* 11 (March 2023): 221.

103. R. N. Winget, D. M. Rees, and G. C. Collett, "Preliminary Investigation of the Brine Flies in the Great Salt Lake, Utah," in *Proceedings of the Twenty-Second Annual Meeting of the Utah Mosquito Abatement Association* (1969): 16–18.

104. Barrett, "Invertebrates and Phytoplankton," 145–73; David B. Herbst, "Biogeography and Physiological Adaptations of the Brine Fly Genus *Ephydra* (Diptera: Ephydridae) in Saline Waters of the Great Basin," *Great Basin Naturalist* (1999): 127–35.

105. Sorensen, "Great Salt Lake Shorebirds," 263–309; Collins, "Population Ecology of *Ephydra*," 99–112.
106. Belovsky, "Great Salt Lake Ecosystem," 1–40.
107. Sorensen, "Great Salt Lake Shorebirds," 263–309.
108. Thomas W. Aldrich and Don S. Paul, "Avian Ecology of Great Salt Lake," in *Great Salt Lake: an Overview of Change*, ed. Wallace J. Gwynn (Utah Geologic Survey, 2002), 343–74; Sorensen, "Great Salt Lake Shorebirds," 263–309.
109. Aldrich, "Avian Ecology," 343–374; J. N. Caudell and M. R. Conover, "Energy Content and Digestibility of Brine Shrimp (*Artemia franciscana*) and Other Prey Items of Eared Grebes (*Podiceps nigricollis*) on the Great Salt Lake, Utah," *Biological Conservation* 130, no. 2 (2006): 251–54; Conover, "Great Salt Lake to Pelagic Birds," 239–62.
110. Caudell, "Energy Content and Digestibility of Prey Items," 251–54; Conover, "Great Salt Lake to Pelagic Birds," 239–62; Anthony J. Roberts, "Avian Diets in a Saline Ecosystem: Great Salt Lake, Utah, USA," *Human-Wildlife Interactions* 7, no. 1 (2013): 158–68; Josh L. Vest and Michael R. Conover, "Food Habits of Wintering Waterfowl on the Great Salt Lake, Utah," *Waterbirds* 34, no. 1 (2011): 40–50; Maureen G. Frank and Michael R. Conover, "Threatened Habitat at Great Salt Lake: Importance of Shallow-Water and Brackish Habitats to Wilson's and Red-Necked Phalaropes," *Condor* 121, no. 2 (2019): 1–13.
111. Vest, "Food Habits of Wintering Waterfowl," 40–50.
112. Frank, "Threatened Phalarope Habitat," 1–13; Sorensen, "Great Salt Lake Shorebirds," 263–309.
113. Pablo Sabat, "Birds in Marine and Saline Environments: Living in Dry Habitats," *Revista Chilena de Historia Natural*, no. 73 (2010): 243–52.
114. Knut Schmidt-Nielsen, "Salt Glands," *Scientific American* 200, no. 1 (1959): 109–19; Malcolm Peaker and James Lincoln Linzell, *Salt Glands in Birds and Reptiles* (Cambridge University Press, 1975)
115. David L. Goldstein, "Renal and Extrarenal Regulation of Body Fluid Composition," in *Sturkie's Avian Physiology* (Academic Press, 2022), 411–43.
116. Jorge S. Gutiérrez, "Living in Environments with Contrasting Salinities: A Review of Physiological and Behavioural Responses in Waterbirds," *Ardeola* 61, no. 2 (2014): 233–56.
117. Jorge S. Gutiérrez et al., "Effects of Salinity on the Immune Response of an 'Osmotic Generalist' Bird," *Oecologia* 171 (2013): 61–69.
118. Kristina M. Hannam, Lewis W. Oring, and Mark P. Herzog, "Impacts of Salinity on Growth and Behavior of American Avocet Chicks," *Waterbirds* 26, no. 1 (2003): 119–25.
119. Joseph R. Jehl, Annette E. Henry, and Judy St. Leger, "Waterbird Mortality in Hypersaline Environments: The Wyoming Trona Ponds," *Hydrobiologia* 697 (2012): 23–29.

120. Great Salt Lake Salinity Advisory Committee, "Influence of Salinity,";
     Zhijun Ma et al., "Managing Wetland Habitats for Waterbirds: An
     International Perspective," *Wetlands* 30 (2010): 15–27.
121. Baxter, "Climate Change," 23–52.
122. Tran, "*Dunaliella viridis* Markers," 118–26.
123. Lindsay, "Salinity Microbialite-Associated Production," e02611.
124. Yang, "Genomic Survey Euhalothece," 1–11.
125. Christophe Dupraz et al., "Processes of Carbonate Precipitation in
     Modern Microbial Mats," *Earth-Science Reviews* 96, no. 3 (2009): 141–62.
126. Steven R. Ahrendt et al., "Effects of Elevated Carbon Dioxide and Salinity
     on the Microbial Diversity in Lithifying Microbial Mats," *Minerals* 4, no. 1
     (2014): 145–69.
127. Anamarija Kolda et al., "How Environment Selects: Resilience and
     Survival of Microbial Mat Community within Intermittent Karst Spring
     Krčić (Croatia)," *Ecohydrology* 12, no. 2 (2019): e2063.
128. Frantz, "Desiccation of Microbialites," 2023.
129. Lindsay, "Microbialite Salinity Gradient," 131–45.
130. Marden, "Great Salt Lake *Artemia*," 175–237.
131. Belovsky, "Great Salt Lake Ecosystem," 1–40.
132. Wei Zhao et al., "The Potential Roles of the G1LEA and G3LEA Proteins
     in Early Embryo Development and in Response to Low Temperature and
     High Salinity in *Artemia sinica*," *PLOS One* 11, no. 9 (2016): e0162272.
133. F. Ono et al., "Life of *Artemia* under Very High Pressure," *Journal of
     Physics and Chemistry of Solids* 71, no. 8 (2010): 1127–30.
134. Herbst, "Salinity Controls in Mojave Desert Ponds," 475–85.
135. Herbst, "Costs of Osmoregulation," 221.
136. Richard Karban and Mikaela Huntzinger, "Spatial and Temporal Refugia
     for an Insect Population Declining Due to Climate Change," *Ecosphere* 12,
     no. 11 (2021): e03820; Gunnar Keppel et al., "Refugia: Identifying and
     Understanding Safe Havens for Biodiversity under Climate
     Change," *Global Ecology and Biogeography* 21, no. 4 (2012): 393–404.
137. Meg A. Krawchuk et al., "Disturbance Refugia within Mosaics of Forest
     Fire, Drought, and Insect Outbreaks," *Frontiers in Ecology and the
     Environment* 18, no. 5 (2020): 235–44.
138. Saccò, "Review Ecology Hypersaline Ecosystems," 2828–50.
139. Marcelle Shoop, "Updating Utah Water Policies for Great Salt
     Lake," *Natural Resources & Environment* 37, no. 3 (2023): 54–55.
140. Great Salt Lake Strike Team, "Enhancing Utah's Strategies to Increase
     Water Levels to Great Salt Lake," https://gardner.utah.edu/great-salt-lake-
     strike-team/, accessed November 2, 2023.

Acknowledgments

This work was a collaboration with a talented science writer and illustrator, Sheila A. Homburger, who provided the graphics for this manuscript. Her illustrations communicate challenging science concepts, and I am grateful for her powerful visuals that accompany my words. Carly Biedul, the Great Salt Lake Institute Coordinator, and Sheila both edited the text, and I appreciate how their feedback made this a better volume. Thanks to all who are working so hard to save Great Salt Lake before it's too late. Your dedication gives me hope.

About the Author

Photo credit: Adam Finkle/ajfphoto.com

Bonnie K. Baxter is a professor of biology and director of Great Salt Lake Institute at Westminster University. Baxter's work has been funded by the National Science Foundation, the National Institutes of Health, NASA, and many private foundations. She has published dozens of scientific articles, but she also enjoys writing for the public. She recently co-edited and co-authored the first academic book on the biology of Great Salt Lake, *Great Salt Lake Biology: A Terminal Lake in a Time of Change*. She also co-wrote the first children's book about this lake, *The Great Great Salt Lake Monster Mystery*. Baxter's research focuses on the lake's extreme microbiology, leading to projects on the lake ecosystem and the limits of life in salt. Her recent studies on microbialites demonstrate the devastating impacts of a shrinking salt lake.